These 4 financial changes will enable me to save almost $6,000 by 2023

JENNIFER VARGAS

Table of Contents

<u>*Summarry*</u>

Major points.

Cutting monthly fees or other recurring expenses could result in significant annual savings for you.

Regularly having no-spend weeks may sound intimidating, but we eased the constraints to make it possible.

Particularly if you live or work overseas, bank fees can build up quickly.

Always check in on your finances towards the end of the year to make sure you're on track. Reducing your monthly expenses can have a significant impact on your bank account at a time when inflation is driving up living costs and a potential recession is looming. In just a few hours, I made savings totaling

over $6,000 for 2023. I did as follows.

Chapter 1

1. Stop subscribing.

- It's time to come clean: I love subscriptions, particularly the ones that give you a specific number of free weeks or a discount for the first six months. The issue is that they can mount up quickly.

I can excuse part of that spending since I conduct a lot of research as a journalist. However, when I looked, I discovered that I was a subscriber to over ten different news and investment websites. That's not all, either. Additionally, I have several streaming services that I seldom ever use as well as a few subscriptions to online education that I would describe as "aspirational."

I've reduced all of these to their bare minimum and may decide to re-subscribe to a few as 2023 goes on. But starting from scratch allows me to continue with the websites I frequent and ignore the others. Additionally, canceling can result in significant savings. To keep you as a customer, some businesses offer large reductions; one claimed to lower the monthly charge from $40 to $10. I just spent an hour online and on the phone to save more than $125 a month, or more than $1,500 annually.

Subscriptions might not be your spending weakness. Use a budgeting program or simply sit down with your most recent bank statements to evaluate your spending patterns; either way, it could have a significant impact on your bottom line the following year.

☐ Here's How to Cancel Subscriptions You Forgot About to Stop Wasting Money on Subscriptions

Consider this study to get an idea of how you might forget your subscriptions. According to a survey of 2,500 people, Americans spend on average $237 a month on subscription services. The number of persons who were unaware of their spending was worrying, even though the amount was rather high:

2100 respondents to the poll, some by as much as $400, overestimated their payments.

☐ How to Terminate Lost Subscriptions

Do you know how much you are paying in subscription fees? In actuality, your expenses are probably much higher than you realize. Keeping track of all the sly subscriptions is challenging, and automatic billing systems make matters even more difficult. Let's examine how to terminate several types of popular subscriptions.

☐ **Device/Smartphone Subscriptions**

Subscriptions obtained through mobile apps are simpler to overlook. These are subscriptions obtained through the iOS App Store or the Play Store for mobile devices. These subscriptions have the advantage that Google and Apple maintain track of payments made through your account (s).

Android: The "Play Store" icon will appear on your device. Tap the "Menu" button in the top left corner (3 horizontal line icons). This will bring up a screen where you can select the individual "Account" that concerns you. To obtain a list of all the services you are paying for, tap on "Subscriptions." Any service that you no longer require can be canceled from here. For more information on this, see Google support.

☐ **Apple:**

To access the iTunes & App Store, open Settings and then select your name. Click on your "Apple ID" link, then select "View Apple ID" and then "Subscriptions." Open the relevant subscription from this screen, then select "Cancel Subscription." The subscription will end after the current billing cycle if you cancel it. Visit Apple support to learn more about managing subscriptions on different iOS devices.

☐ **Utilize tools for tracking subscriptions**

These are online resources and applications for tracking your expenditure in real-time. They operate by reviewing your bank records and giving you a list of the services that are being charged to your account (s).

Rocket Money helps you stop paying for subscriptions you no longer require by identifying your subscriptions. When you need to cancel undesirable subscriptions, your concierge is available to do it for you.

A software called Truebill keeps track of all subscriptions, including Netflix and Club memberships. Additionally, it analyzes percentage shifts in the prices charged for each item. Simply tap the cancel button on the subscription you want to cancel.

Although Trim is an online application and the cancellation is done by text, it functions similarly.

The app Empower follows the same pattern. It displays the costs associated with each service as well as account balances for things like bank accounts, Amazon, Uber, AT&T Wireless, etc. With this information, getting in touch to cancel or renegotiate specific subscriptions is simple.

☐ **Popular Websites Online**

How do I cancel my subscription to Onlyfans?

A content subscription service called OnlyFans makes it possible for content producers to share their work. You can cancel your subscriptions in two different methods. Open your OnlyFans account and log in first if you already have one. Find the "User's profile" you want to delete by searching for it. then deactivate Auto-Renew. Before completing the procedure, confirm. Sending support an email is the second option. From their end, they will assist you in canceling the membership.

☐ **How to stop your subscription to ProBiller**

An online merchant gateway for several subscription services is called ProBiller. If you noticed a charge from ProBiller on your account, it was probably made through one of their merchants. You can get more information about the website the subscription is through by contacting ProBiller if you're unclear. Call the ProBiller customer support line to cancel your subscriptions. then ask to speak with a customer service representative. Make sure you are prepared with all of your account information. Give the representative your account information and the details of the service you want to stop receiving. If necessary, request a fee refund and ask them to send you an email confirming the cancellation.

☐ How to end subscriptions to Cashapp

Users of the CashApp mobile app can send money to others. Users using iPhone and iPad devices should click on their names under the app's settings. Then select "Subscriptions" from the menu. Go to iTunes and the Appstore for assistance if you are unable to find the choice right away. Once the "Subscription" has expired, sign in with your Apple ID by clicking on it, then scroll down to find the "Subscription" option. After that, select the "CashApp" (subscription) you want to cancel by clicking it. If you are unable to find the cancellation option, the subscription has probably been successfully terminated.

Users of Android devices should visit Google Playstore, hit the menu, then select "Subscriptions," and Click "cancel subscription" after selecting the "Cashapp subscription" that needs to be ended.

☐ Manual Subscriptions and Email

Not every subscription comes from an app store. On your computer, it's simple to locate any lapsed subscriptions that you may have created years ago. The same is true for manual subscription forms that are filled out at fairs, streets, malls, etc. The subscription alerts could arrive as spam mail (which, let's face it, you never read).

Searching through your emails for any subscriptions is the best course of action. Send an email to the service providers to cancel the subscriptions. If this is difficult to find, look through your bank statements from the previous 12 months. Watch out for forgotten or false regular subscriptions. You can cancel them by emailing the relevant businesses or by visiting the associated websites.

Is There a Simpler Way to Stop Subscriptions?

Going through bank records that might or might not include subscriptions doesn't sound all that fun. Smart gadget subscriptions are even more difficult to monitor because your children may occasionally tap on a new one or buy something in-app. Is there a simple way to accomplish this? There is.

□ **To round up this important update up**

It's simple to have unwanted and fraudulent subscriptions drain your bank account. The issue gets worse as automated payment systems come online. To find these payments, go through your bills and bank statements. On smart devices, you may also use the "Cancel Subscription" option. Utilizing internet tools and apps to keep track of and terminate unwanted subscriptions is a much simpler

method.

Chapter 2

2. Regularly scheduled no-spend weeks.

- I saved more than $200 during my first no-spend week earlier this year. In 2023, my partner and I will perform our rendition during the final week of each month.

What is meant by "our version"? We will reduce our non-essential spending, but we will still attend birthday parties or other special events. It makes sense that you could believe that is cheating.

Our biggest challenge in establishing a regular no-spend week was not socializing. We concluded that if keeping to a rigorous monthly no-spend week meant disappointing friends or skipping crucial social events, we wouldn't do it. It is preferable to design an exception that makes it possible then to do nothing at all. Total savings for the upcoming year? I'm estimating it will cost a modest $150 per month or $1,800 annually.

Chapter 3

3. I modified my banking practices.

- I live abroad, which frequently makes my banking position more difficult.

For instance, I do not meet the requirements for many of the best credit cards available to Americans. If I'm not careful, my regular transactions will result in large foreign costs. Since my bank's regulations changed this year, for instance, I no longer receive free foreign transactions (I now pay over 2% to use my card). Additionally, I have to pay 5% to get some client payments.

All of this implies that I could improve my banking practices and save at least $250 each month. I've established enough credit history in Colombia, where I currently reside, to qualify for a rewards credit card. I'm converting to a bank account designed for persons with international addresses. And I've discovered ways to lower the fees I pay on money I receive. That totals a staggering $3,000 in additional savings.

If you don't live or work abroad, changing your banking practices could result in less significant savings. However, even a small monthly expense reduction of $20 or $30 might add up. Examine the bank fees you are now paying to see whether you could change checking accounts and save money. Or perhaps switching to a different savings account might yield better results. If you look, you can find a credit card that better suits your spending patterns. Or perhaps you'll realize that the annual fee on your credit card is no longer necessary. As we all struggle with the inflationary crisis, every little bit counts.

Chapter 4

4. I automated my investment process.

- Being a freelancer, I've always been hesitant to set up an automatic transfer to my brokerage account because I can never be certain of how much money I'll make.

I wish to invest more money next year because it is one of the best ways to accumulate wealth.

Based on my present salary, I've set some potentially attainable investment goals for myself. I can avoid having to think about making such recurring contributions by setting up automated payments. Furthermore, I have no intention of using that money for anything else. And I'll adjust the transfer amount if my financial status changes.

It's impossible to predict how much money I'll save by automating my investments because so much depends on the performance of the stock market. Theoretically, because of compound interest, every dollar I put in the upcoming year could be worth significantly more in ten or twenty years. The goal of this financial decision is to prioritize long-term wealth creation over short-term savings.

☐ How to Make Your Investments Automatic.

a methodical plan for automating your investment strategy.

When it comes to saving for retirement, many people have the best of intentions. However, even the best-laid plans can go wrong, particularly if your investing practices aren't as regular as grocery shopping or bill paying.

You can automate your investing tasks to prevent falling short of your financial objectives, which might postpone your retirement. Automation makes sure that you keep investing at a regular rate even when you initially have to put in more work. Learn the five simple steps for automating investments.

☐ **You may automate your financial decisions by doing the following five simple things:**

☐ *__Automate investments in a retirement account provided by the business__*

A 401(k) or other work-related retirement plan is one of the simplest automatic investment alternatives (k). If your employer provides this benefit, take full advantage of it. Try to maximize your company's matching contribution, at the very least. Numerous employers will match between 50% and 100% of your contributions, up to a set proportion of your pay. You lose out on a portion of your overall compensation if you don't take advantage of this chance. You've also assisted in automating your money by ensuring that you receive your full work retirement benefit.

Before you hit the 2023 401(k) contribution limitations of $19,500 or $26,000 if you're 50 or older, the majority of employer matches will have run their course. However, if you enjoy your investment selections, that doesn't imply you can't maximize this plan. This is a smart approach to making regular stock market investments.

☐ ***Combine all of your accounts for investments.***

Every five years on average, people change employment. Unfortunately, lots of people leave their 401(k)s behind. According to the Center for Retirement Research at Boston College, Americans have amassed $1.35 trillion in assets in 24 million former 401(k) plans from previous employment.

Even though it could be a pain, rolling over an old 401(k) into an IRA has several advantages:

It is simpler to manage your investment portfolio when all of your previous workplace-related retirement accounts are combined into one account.

Given that certain 401(k) plans have greater costs, it might save you money.

If you kept your old 401(k) assets in a lower-return investment, your returns might increase.

If you have investment accounts with different brokers, you might think about merging them as well as your previous work-related retirement funds. Your investment will be simpler and easier to automate if everything is in one location.

Additionally, now is the ideal time to think about establishing new automatic investment accounts. For instance, if you have children, you might want to create a 529 plan to help you save money for college costs. Additionally, check to see whether you qualify for a health savings account (HSA).

Summarry

- Everyone has a varied financial condition, and some of us keep things tighter than others.

Everyone hates squandering money, whether it's on pointless bank fees or subscriptions they hardly ever use. Review your spending patterns for a few hours to determine how much you can cut back on next year; you might be surprised.